# BEARS

## MYTHS AND LEGENDS

*Translated by* Frances Halton

*Text by* Bernard Briais

*Illustrations by* François Davot

*Series edited by* Gilles Ragache

CHERRYTREE BOOKS

A Cherrytree Book

Adapted by A S Publishing
from *Les Ours*
published by Hachette


First published 1995
by Cherrytree Press Ltd
a subsidiary of
The Chivers Company Ltd
Windsor Bridge Road
Bath, Avon BA2 3AX



British Library Cataloguing in Publication Data
Briais, Bernard
Bears.—(Myths and Legends Series)
I. Halton, Frances II. Briais, Bernard
III. Series
398.2452974446

ISBN 0-7451-5260-0

Printed in Hong Kong by Colorcraft Ltd

forgot all about Mielikki and his promise. At first he used his pointed teeth and sharp claws to attack small animals in play, but as he grew more aware of his strength he took on larger opponents. And he always won. At last he reached a village and attacked the people who lived there. They had never seen a bear and ran off in terror. But their children were not fast enough to escape Otso's teeth and claws.

Otso had not realized that, although people were weak, their weapons could hurt him. Too late, he remembered the promise he had made to Mielikki. Too late, he understood that from now on he would never be able to live in peace, for people, who were weaker but cleverer than him, would always be his enemies.

*Mielikki doted on Otso, the baby bear.*

CANADA

# THE MASTER OF LIGHT

Once upon a time a great bear ruled the world above the sky. It kept all the light and heat in the universe jealously for itself. Meanwhile Earth was in unbroken darkness, blanketed in snow and raked by an icy wind. Many animals died from cold and hunger.

The desperate animals set out to search for the highest tree they could find. At last, on the top of a mountain, they found an immense fir, the tip of which was hidden by the clouds. They sent the nimble squirrel to climb it. Higher and higher it scrambled through the branches, waving its bushy tail to clear its way through the thick cloud. Little by little the mists above its head thinned, until it was blinded by a brilliant light. It had broken through the vault of the sky and entered the world above.

Gradually the squirrel's eyes adapted to the light, until it was able to see an enormous bear, asleep on an island under a strange tree. From the tree's branches hung curious fruit, like waterskins shimmering with heat. 'If I could take back just one of those fruits, our troubles on Earth would be ended,' thought the squirrel.

The squirrel made its way down through the clouds until it could signal to the other animals to join it. Some of them climbed the tree quite easily, but others found it difficult. It was a long time before they arrived in the world above. 'Which of us would be able to pick one of the burning fruits?' asked the squirrel. 'Which of us is a good enough swimmer to reach the island? Which of us is strong enough to confront the huge bear and carry back the heavy fruit, and swift enough to escape from its claws and teeth?'

*The reindeer rushed ahead of the great bear, keeping its precious burden safe.*

The animals talked this over for a long time. The hare ran fast but could not swim. The beaver was an excellent swimmer, but it was not strong enough to tackle the bear. Then the squirrel noticed the reindeer which hovered timidly on the edge of the group. It alone could carry out the dangerous mission. As fast a swimmer as it was on land, it had formidable antlers on its head. All the animals agreed.

The reindeer set off to swim to the island. When it was half way there, it heard a squeaky voice in its ear. The voice came from a mouse that had hidden in the reindeer's fur. The reindeer was annoyed, but it was too late to turn back.

As soon as it reached the island, the reindeer rushed towards the tree from which hung the incandescent fruit. Before the bear realized what was happening, the reindeer loaded a fruit on to its back and set off. The furious bear reached the shore and climbed into its canoe, paddling with all its might in pursuit. The reindeer, hampered by its load, made slow progress. It called to the mouse, but there was no reply. 'Poor little mouse,' it thought, 'I ran too fast; it must have fallen off on the island.'

The exhausted reindeer looked back to see the bear's canoe gaining inexorably. Just when all hope seemed lost, the bear's paddle broke in its paws. The mouse had crept into the canoe and had gnawed through the paddle with its sharp teeth. It used a piece of the paddle as a raft to float triumphantly back to its friends.

Heat from the fruit melted the ice and snow which covered the Earth, and the hole pierced by the squirrel through the sky to the light became the sun. If it does not shine every day, this is because the bear's dark fur sometimes covers it, but the ruler of the sky always goes back to its island in the end.

## FINLAND

# THE SON OF THE SKY

Ever since he was born, the little bear, son of the God of the Skies, had looked down through the clouds to the world that was dimly visible below. When he grew bored with his carefree life he dreamed of visiting this world. The more his father tried to warn him of its dangers, the more impatient he became. He began to mope, growing sad and listless.

'If you go down to Earth, you will never be able to climb back to the Sky again,' warned his father. But the little bear took no notice. At last, worn out by his son's pleas, the God of the Skies gave in. An immense iron chain was lowered to the Earth's surface and the young bear slid down it. As he drew near he could see hills and forests, lakes and valleys. It was a wonderful, endlessly varied world.

The bear landed in the middle of a meadow. It was high summer, and he easily found berries, honey and fruit to eat. But before long the trees changed colour, and their leaves fell. Winter arrived with snow and bitter winds. In spite of his fur, the bear was very cold. Food became scarce and the bear learned what it was to be hungry. No one in the sky had taught him to hunt, so he wandered about with an empty belly and a frozen nose. He wished he had never left his father but dared not ask him for help until he realized that his only alternative was to die.

The God of the Skies decided that his son had been punished enough by cold and hunger. He gave him a bow and arrows and showed him how to use them. And he taught him how to light a fire to keep warm.

'I hope,' he said sternly, 'that your troubles have taught you a little sense. As you have to live on Earth, I shall entrust you with a noble mission. In my name you must see that there is justice and peace among people. You must protect those who are weak, good and honest, and punish those who are wicked, those who cheat, lie, steal and harm others.'

The bear thanked his father for his trust and promised that he would be worthy of it. But the God of the Skies was mistaken; his son had learned nothing. He showed favour to those who flattered him and who pandered to his greed. His goodwill could be bought with a honeycomb. The God of the Skies was furious. He gave people permission to hunt his son just like any other animal. They waited until he was asleep and killed him. Then they took possession of the bow and the fire with which the God of the Skies had entrusted him.

*The young bear slid to Earth down a vast chain to land in a meadow of flowers.*

*The fox sloped off as the villagers' dogs attacked the trapped bear.*

LAPLAND

# HOW THE BEAR LOST HIS TAIL

The fox gnawed contentedly at a trout, stolen an hour earlier from a Lapp's larder. It was a long time since he had had such a feast and he took his time, savouring each mouthful.

A passing bear smelt the fish. Winter had taken him by surprise and he was wandering about with an empty stomach, dragging his tail behind him. In those far-off days bears had long, bushy tails, as splendid as those of foxes and wolves. The bear's first thought was to charge at the fox and snatch away the fish. But the fox had already seen him, and if it came to a chase the bear would never catch him. So he asked the fox politely if he could have a taste – just a tiny mouthful – of the fish.

'It's so long since I've eaten one that I've forgotten what it's like,' he said plaintively.

'If you want to eat fish, go and catch some like me!' snarled the fox.

'Fish in weather like this?' replied the bear. 'All the lakes and rivers are iced over.'

'Quite!' said the fox. 'That's the ideal time.'

The bear looked dumbfounded, so the fox went on. 'They say many hard things about us foxes, but I'll show you that we don't deserve our bad reputation. I shall teach you how to fish in winter. First choose a clear, starlit night. Make your way to a lake or pond and dig a hole in the ice. The fish will be drawn to it by the starlight. So, never mind the cold, plunge your tail into the water and wait. You will feel the fish catching hold of your tail one by one. When there are enough to make a good meal, pull up your tail, and there you are!'

'In fact,' said the bear thoughtfully, 'any animal could do that.'

'Even the most stupid,' agreed the fox, 'so long as it has a long tail.'

The next night was cold and clear, and the stars lit up the sky. Despite the piercing cold, the bear set out for the nearest lake. The ice was so thick that it was difficult to make a hole, but at last he succeeded and plunged his tail into the freezing water. He shivered until his teeth chattered, but how else could he get any food?

Nothing disturbed the silence of the night. The bear waited. Then suddenly he saw a shadowy figure drawing near. It was his new friend, the fox.

'Are you coming fishing, too?' asked the bear.

'No, not tonight; I've fish enough in store. But it certainly is a wonderful night for fishing.'

'I think my tail is growing heavy,' said the bear. 'That must be the first fish biting,' said the fox. 'Wait a little!'

'My tail is growing heavier and heavier. If I wait too long, I won't be able to pull it up,' wailed the bear.

'Don't worry, I'll be here to give you a hand,' the fox reassured him. 'It's best to stock up for a good while.'

The fox waited until the bear's tail was firmly frozen into the ice. Then it set out for the nearest village. There it stirred up a fearful racket, frightening the chickens and waking the dogs and the villagers. Everyone chose a weapon and rushed towards the fox. He waited until they had nearly reached him and then set off, leading them straight to the lake, where the poor bear was stuck in the ice. When the villagers saw the huge beast, they rushed at him, quite forgetting the fox!

The bear tugged desperately at the ice round his tail until at last he broke free. He just escaped his attackers, but he had to leave his magnificent tail behind in the ice. And that, say the Lapps, is why bears today have such silly, short tails.

*Sweat poured off the bear
as he rested by the viper
in the sun.*

## CANADA

# THE BEAR AND THE SNAKE

Fire had destroyed everything. The Earth was a vast desert. As far as the eye could see, there was nothing but rocks blackened by the blaze, and smoking tree stumps. There was no sign of life; the animals had burned or suffocated in the smoke.

A single distraught bear wandered about. Deep in the shelter of his cave, he had escaped the blaze. For days he searched despairingly for some other living creature. At last he thought he saw movement far off on a hillside. The bear ran to the hill as fast as possible. There he found himself nose to nose with a viper. The bear cried out happily: he was no longer alone! The female viper, who had escaped the fire by sheltering at the bottom of a river, was pleased to find the bear. Since they might well be the only survivors of the great catastrophe, the bear and the snake decided to join forces and live together. Nothing could be worse than being alone.

When evening came, the bear suggested to his new friend that they should sleep in his large, comfortable cave. But the snake refused: 'No, what is the point of tiring ourselves out by going so far. See this hole in the ground – this is an ideal lodging for me!' And without waiting, she slithered into the hole and fell fast asleep. Of course the bear could not possibly follow her. The hole was so small that he could not even get a paw into it. He was taken aback, but, as he did not want to lose his new friend, he lay down in the open.

The bear woke early after a very uncomfortable night and decided to prepare a surprise for the viper. He had noticed nearby a thicket that had miraculously been spared by the fire. First he collected the finest berries to make the snake a splendid meal. 'Look!' he said proudly to the snake when she poked her head out of the hole. 'Now you can have a feast.'

But the snake just pulled a cross face when she saw the berries. 'I'll go and find something to eat for myself,' she grumbled, and slithered off beneath some thorny bushes where the bear could not follow.

The bear asked himself what he could do to please his friend. He tried to play with her, but when he patted her with his giant paw he scratched her with his claws. She hissed and flicked her forked tongue at him, and he sprang back in fright.

Towards midday, the snake wanted to sleep. The bear thought this a splendid idea, since he was tired after his uncomfortable night. The snake curled up on a rock in the sun. The bear timidly suggested that they found some shade. 'I'm fine where I am,' hissed the snake. 'Settle down near me if you want to chat.' So the bear, wanting to please her, sat down in the sun. His thick fur made him so hot that sweat poured off him. When he felt that he was about to suffocate from heat, he said to the snake: 'My friend, don't you see that I shall die of sunstroke if I stay here? Let's find a little shade.'

'It's not my fault if your fur is too thick,' hissed the snake grumpily. 'I'm perfectly happy here.' But the bear could stand the heat no longer. He got up and plodded towards some nearby rocks where there was some lifegiving shade. When he was feeling better, he mused out loud to himself: 'The snake will not live in my cave, and she will not eat my food. She likes the sun while I love the shade. In fact, we are different in every way and we shall never live happily together.' With a last look at the snake, the bear set off towards the horizon. It would be better to be alone than to have such an uncomfortable companion!

## CANADA

# THE BEAR, THE TURTLE AND THE MARMOT

Winter lasts a long time in the forests of northern Canada. And so Makwa the bear looked for a friend to share his cave during the dreary, sunless months. But the caribou was off on a long journey south, the wolf was leaving with his family, and the white-headed eagle did not want to come down to land.

Makwa was plodding gloomily beside a swamp when he saw a large, round pebble. 'I hear you are looking for company during the winter,' murmured the strange stone. 'I'll share your cave. My name is Makikinak.'

The startled bear saw the pebble move; it had four feet and a strange, bald head at the end of a thick, straight neck. It was a turtle. 'What an odd creature,' thought the bear. 'But who cares what it looks like if it will keep me company.'

And so the bear and the turtle set off towards Makwa's cave, for the first snowflakes were beginning to fall and the sun was low on the horizon. When they arrived, the new friends settled down comfortably for the winter. Most of the time they slept.

Weeks and then months passed, until one day Makwa decided to leave the cave and see what was happening. Next day, when he returned, he said that there was no sign of spring. He went out several more times, and when he got back he always told the impatient turtle that winter seemed to be lasting for ever!

One day when the bear was snoring beside the fire after one of his excursions, the turtle glimpsed traces of myrtleberries on his teeth. The bear had been lying! The furious turtle put her nose out of the cave and saw that the snow had melted and spring was far advanced.

'That wretched bear will pay for this,' she said. She stopped up the mouth of the cave with branches and set them alight. The bear, roused by the smoke, rushed coughing to the entrance, and burned his nose as he pushed through. The turtle took shelter in the nearest swamp.

Summer followed spring, and then autumn came round once more. Food became scarce. One day the bear caught the scent of raspberries from a little island in a lake. He flung himself impatiently into the water and began to swim towards it, when suddenly he felt something attach itself to one of his back paws and drag him down. When he plunged his head under water to see what was happening he saw that Makikinak was gripping on to his fur with her sharp beak.

Bears are good swimmers, but the turtle pulled with all her strength. Just as the bear reached the island, part of his paw, cut through by the turtle's beak, dropped down to the lake bottom. There it wriggled and then began to swim. A new animal – the marmot – had been formed! And this is why, say the people who live by Hudson Bay, marmots, like bears, hibernate in winter.

*The turtle clung so tightly to the bear's hind paw that he could not shake her off.*

*Arcas was about to shoot when his father Zeus intervened.*

## GREECE

# THE GREAT BEAR AND THE LITTLE BEAR

Artemis, goddess of the hunt, was strict with her followers. When she learned that her faithful companion, the nymph Callisto, had secretly had a baby, she immediately turned her away from her court – even though the baby's father was none other than Zeus, king of the gods and master of Olympus!

Poor Callisto sat down by a fountain and wondered what would become of her. She dared not go home to her father, King Lycaon, in the Peloponnese. Meanwhile, on top of Mount Olympus, Zeus's wife Hera had learned of her husband's latest exploit. When she saw Callisto leaning tenderly over her little son, Arcas, Hera's blood boiled; she took her revenge by turning her rival into a bear and condemning her to wander for ever with the wild mountain animals.

Watched over from afar by his father Zeus, Arcas grew to be a handsome youth with curly hair and dark eyes. One day he went to his grandfather, King Lycaon. The boy was received with open arms, and taught Lycaon's subjects how to sew corn, to bake bread and weave woollen cloth. In time he succeeded his grandfather and his kingdom flourished.

When he could find time Arcas loved to hunt in the mountains. One day, he followed the tracks of a shebear. Strangely, instead of running from him, the bear seemed to wait for him. It was Callisto, who wanted to see her son. When he was within a short distance, Arcas drew his bow and carefully aimed his arrow. Just as he was letting fly, Zeus, realizing the impending tragedy, stayed his arm and turned him into a bear as well. Then he carried Callisto and Arcas into the sky, where they can be seen to this day as the constellations the Great Bear and the Little Bear.

LAPLAND

# THE INQUISITIVE WOMAN

Every autumn, old Skolte disappeared. He stayed away until spring, and no one dared ask him where he spent the winter months.

One year his daughter-in-law decided to follow him at a distance, taking care not to be seen. The light powdering of snow that covered the ground showed his tracks clearly. After a time, she saw him. The old man seemed to be searching for something, looking carefully at the trees around him. At last he stopped by a fir, the tip of which bent sharply towards the north.

Old Skolte dropped on all fours and crawled round the treetrunk three times. By the end of the third time, he had turned into an old, grey-muzzled bear! The astonished girl watched the bear go on his way and went up to the tree. She could not resist dropping on all fours and imitating her father-in-law. And she too turned into a bear – but one with beautiful glossy fur! At first she was delighted, but before long she wanted to be human again. She went to Skolte, who was sheltering in a nearby cave, and asked him how she could do this. When he saw her, the old bear flew into a rage.

'You stupid girl,' he yelled, 'now you must spend all winter here; you cannot shed your bear's skin until spring! If you go home like this, your husband is bound to shoot you.' When she heard this, the girl began to wail like a bear caught in a trap.

'What's the good of moaning?' asked old Skolte. 'You should have thought before you acted. Now all you can do is wait. Do as I do – lie down and sleep.' And for the next few months they stayed snug in their cave.

When the snow began to melt they left the cave and old Skolte turned towards a stream. 'To get back your human form,' he told his daughter-in-law, 'you must jump over the water. When you land on the other side, you will be a woman again.'

Old Skolte jumped first, and easily cleared the stream. The girl followed, but she missed her footing and one of her paws splashed in the water. As a result she never completely regained her human form. For the rest of her life, she had one pretty foot and one bear's paw, complete with claws. 'Serves her right for being so nosy!' said the Lapps.

*For the rest of her life, the poor woman had to limp along with one bear's paw.*

*A mysterious pale lady, crowned with flowers and draped in veils, appeared to the Moor and signed to him to follow her.*

# ANDORRA

## ▷ THE BEAR THAT LIMPED ◁

It was the time of the Crusades, when Muslims and Christians were at war. The whole valley of Valira, the only route through the mountains in Andorra, was controlled by the Moors, who were Muslims. From their fortress of La Cecca, perched on a rocky summit, they raided the countryside and plundered the villages. But they respected the religion of the peasants, who had long been Christians. They spared their churches and their sacred treasures.

One night, however, a greedy and unscrupulous Moorish warrior decided to loot the chapels of Juverri and Auvinya. Although this old soldier had fought for the Islamic religion for more than twenty years, he had no faith and knew no law. He had received many wounds. The worst had left him with a limp.

The night was black as ink; low clouds masked the moon and stifled almost all noise. The soldier's horse picked its way cautiously along the stony path that led to the chapel of Juverri.

Just as the warrior was about to open the door of the chapel, a bell began to ring. Startled, he looked up at the bell tower. It was lit up by a pale cloud, which little by little took the form of a woman, her head crowned with flowers, her shoulders draped with floating veils. She beckoned him gently, and in a strange, sweet voice ordered him to follow her. The frightened soldier felt compelled to obey her. She led him to a spring in the middle of the forest, where she made him swear that he would never again attack holy places.

Night after night, the soldier went back to the mountain, but he never saw the beautiful woman again. He decided that he must have been dreaming. And so he set out once more to loot the chapels. Under cover of darkness, he left La Cecca. At dawn next day, his riderless horse appeared at the gate of the fortress. The warrior was never seen again.

Some years later, the armies of Charlemagne drove the Moors from Andorra. Life in the valleys became peaceful once more. The shepherds had only to fight their age-old enemies, the bears that preyed on their flocks.

A great bear hunt was organized. All the peasants set off with their dogs, but they only found one old, lame bear. It defended itself fiercely, but the odds were overwhelming. As the bear fell, it seemed to say a few words in a language no one could understand.

That night the chief hunter could not sleep. He kept thinking about the bear. Outside, the dogs began to bark. The hunter opened his door and saw, sitting on the side of a well, a beautiful pale lady. He went up to her and she revealed to him that the animal they had killed that day was not like the other mountain bears. Long ago, to punish a Moorish warrier who had wished to steal sacred treasures, she had turned him into a bear and condemned him to wander through the forests until he died.

When they learned this story, the people of Andorra wanted to thank the lady who watched over their mountains and valleys. So they named the great rock between the villages of Juverri and Auvinya the Senyoreta (the young lady). It is just at the place where the Moor was turned into a bear.

RUSSIA

# IVANKA AND THE GENIE OF THE LAKE

'Ivanka! Ivanka!' The villagers called Ivanka's name and clapped their hands in rhythm as Ivanka danced faster and faster among them.

This was one of the sights of the region. People came from far and wide to see the strange creature, who was human down to the waist and bear below. Ivanka, they whispered, had been born in a bear's cave where his mother had taken shelter one winter.

'Ivanka!' A harsh call halted the dancer. Recognizing his father's voice, Ivanka turned towards him, hanging his head in shame. 'I've been looking for you for an hour or more. Go home at once and as you pass the sheep fold collect a sheep for dinner tomorrow.'

'Very well, father!' said Ivanka. 'But which sheep shall I catch?' His father snapped back, 'It doesn't matter. Take whichever looks at you!' So Ivanka set off. When he passed the sheep, all of them turned and looked at him. And so he killed them all! When his father learned that his flock had been destroyed, he was furious. 'That boy is so stupid, he will ruin me,' he raged. So he thought up a way of getting rid of his son.

On the far boundary of his land was a lake at the bottom of which lived a genie who dragged down anyone unwise enough to go near.

'Ivanka,' said his father, 'the tenant of my land by the lake has never paid me any rent. I'd like you to go and collect what is owing.' The boy set off at once. As he drew near the lake, it became hard to see in the greenish light filtering through the tangled branches of the trees. But nothing ever bothered Ivanka. He sat down on the shore of the lake and called out. A hideous genie sprang out of the water. Ivanka, quite undismayed, said cheerfully: 'My name is Ivanka. You are living on my father's land without paying rent.'

'Rent!' gasped the astonished genie. 'You want me to pay rent?' And he burst into peals of devilish laughter. Ivanka was unperturbed. 'You have to pay,' he repeated obstinately. The genie was astonished, but finally said: 'Oh well, all right. I'll pay your father rent, if you can beat me in a race.' For he had seen how slowly and clumsily Ivanka moved. 'That would be too easy,' replied Ivanka cheerfully. 'Even my newborn brother, who is asleep behind that huge oak, could run faster than you. Do you want to race against him?'

'All right,' said the genie, even more amazed at Ivanka's stupidity. 'But, if I win, not only will I refuse to pay the rent, but I will drag you both down to the bottom of the lake.'

Ivanka went over to the oak where he had seen a hare asleep. Pulling gently at its long ears, he woke it up. When the hare saw the genie it set off with all speed. Before the monster began to chase it, the hare was out of sight. 'Very well, I've lost,' acknowledged the genie. 'But you must give me another chance.'

'As you like,' said Ivanka, 'but you must swear by all the devils of the forests and the mountains that if I win, you will pay.' The genie swore this solemn oath and added: 'If you can

*A fearful genie rose from the lake. It would have terrified most people, but Ivanka was not bothered.*

*Ivanka had to make so many journeys to take home the genie's gold that winter set in before he finished.*

throw my stick higher than I can, I'll give in and pay the rent!'

'You throw first,' agreed the boy, and watched as the genie threw the stick so high that it disappeared from sight before falling back to the ground. 'Over to you, Ivanka!' he smirked. Ivanka took the stick in his hand, but then stayed still, gazing at the sky. 'It's your turn, Ivanka; throw the stick!' said the genie impatiently. 'Yes, yes, I know; I'm just waiting until that cloud is over my head. Then I'll throw the stick on to it,' said Ivanka. 'No!' cried the genie. 'Rather than lose my magic stick I will pay the rent to your father. How much does he want?'

'My father is not greedy,' said Ivanka. 'Fill my hat with gold, and that will be enough.' The genie decided that Ivanka must really be the most stupid boy in the whole world. He disappeared into the lake to collect the gold. Meanwhile Ivanka made a hole in the crown of his hat and placed it over a hole he had noticed in the ground. The genie reappeared, carrying a sack full of gold. He tipped it into the hat, but to his surprise the hat remained empty.

'You swore by all the devils of the forests and the mountains,' Ivanka reminded him gently. The genie went off for a second, larger sack of gold, and tipped it into the hat – but still it was empty. 'You swore,' murmured Ivanka. The genie brought sack after sack of gold; but still the hat was not even half full. 'Ivanka, I've given you all my gold and still your hat is empty. What do you wish me to do? Only you can release me from my oath!'

'I will release you from your oath if you leave my father's land for ever and do not settle within a thousand miles of here.' The genie rushed off immediately, and was never seen in that land again. Ivanka went home and fetched a big cart. He had to make so many journeys to carry back the gold that winter came before he had finished!

## RUSSIA

# THE GULLIBLE BEAR

The bear plodded down to the valley to buy lard for the winter. His neighbour the fox saw him set off; he overtook the bear by a short cut, and met up with him as if by chance. 'This is a surprise!' he exclaimed. 'Where are you off to this beautiful morning?'

'I'm off to stock up with lard for the winter,' replied the bear. 'What a coincidence!' said the fox. 'I had the same idea. If we pool our money, we will be able to buy a whole barrel of lard.'

As they spoke, the fox jingled some coins in his pocket. The bear assumed that he had a small fortune and agreed the deal. When the time came to pay for their lard, the fox emptied his pockets: out came three small coins and a great handful of nails!

The bear understood – too late – that he had been fooled. The large barrel of lard he had dreamed of dwindled to the small one he would have had anyway. Furiously he turned on the fox, who retorted: 'Think a little, idiot! How could you carry a heavier barrel than this?'

Once they were back in the mountains, the bear decided to keep the lard in his cave to await the winter. 'Let me sleep in your cave,' insisted the fox. 'I know how greedy you are; you will eat the whole barrel before the first frosts.' The bear disliked his neighbour, but he hated being alone. And so he agreed that the fox could spend the winter in his cave.

The first night, the fox waited until the bear was asleep – and bears are very sound sleepers. Then the fox ate a good helping of lard. Next morning, the bear noticed the fox's round stomach and asked him: 'What were you doing while I was asleep?'

*When autumn came, the bear set off for the village to stock up with lard.*

'Friends from higher up the mountain asked us to the baptism of their new baby. You didn't hear them, and I didn't want to wake you up. We celebrated until the early hours!' said the fox. The bear asked the baby's name. 'It's a very odd name,' said the cunning fox. 'It's to be called Quarter-Barrel.'

The next night just the same happened and the following day, when the bear saw the well-fed fox, he wanted to know where he had been. 'You'll never believe me,' said the fox, 'but friends from lower down the mountain called. They were baptizing their new baby. I didn't want to wake you up so I ate for both of us!' The bear laughed sourly and said, 'I can see that from your bulging stomach. And what is this baby to be called?' Smiling, the fox replied, 'Another strange name – Half-Barrel!'

On the third night, the fox finished up the lard in the barrel. It gave him fearful indigestion. When the bear opened his eyes, he asked his companion why he had not gone out. 'It's because of the third baptism,' said the fox. 'A third baptism?' said the bear suspiciously. 'Yes! I wish I had sent you in my place,' said the fox sadly, 'because now I feel very ill.' This time the bear was even more doubtful. 'A third baptism? And what is the infant's name this time?' With a sly grin, the fox replied, 'It's just as silly a name as the others. The parents have decided to call it Empty-Barrel.'

Even the slow-witted bear realized that the fox was mocking him, and he hurried over to the lard barrel. He was so angry when he found it empty that the whole mountain shook with his growls. He seized a club and rushed towards the

*The bear fell fast asleep in front of the warm fire.*

fox, who turned on him and accused him. 'Thief and rascal!' he screamed. 'While I was out at the baptisms, you scoffed our lard!'

The bear was furious. 'How can you accuse me when you know that you ate all the lard yourself?' he spluttered. 'We can soon prove who's speaking the truth,' said the fox. 'Light the fire, and we will sit with our backs to the hearth. The lard will melt, and whoever has the greasiest fur will be the thief.'

The bear, knowing he was innocent, thought this a good idea. So they both sat down with their backs to the flames. Soon the bear dozed off with the heat – as the fox had expected. He sneaked off to the barrel and scraped out the remaining traces of lard. He melted them in the heat, and rubbed them thickly on his neighbour's back.

When the bear woke up, he saw the fox, apparently sound asleep, at his side. He ran his hand over his thick fur, and found to his astonishment that it was sticky with lard! He looked at the fox's fur which showed no trace of grease. The bewildered bear could not think what had happened. The fox (who had been wide awake the whole time) sat up and accused the bear roundly. 'I knew all the time that you were the thief! Everyone knows that bears can't resist temptation and that greed always gets them. Give me back my money, you villain!'

The bear, asking himself how he could possibly have eaten a whole barrel of lard without knowing it, went to search for his last few coins. The fox took them and sloped off. 'Goodbye!' he called over his shoulder; 'I'm not staying a moment longer with a thief!'

*The polar bear said goodbye to his brother Uluksak.*

## CANADA

# NANOOK THE BROWN AND NANOOK THE WHITE

Everyone in the Inuit village was delighted when Atitak, Anakattak's wife, gave birth to twin boys. But Atitak tucked her head under the covers and cried inconsolably. For her babies were covered from head to toe with hair so thick that she could hardly even make out their little twinkling eyes.

As he tried to calm his wife, Anakattak busied himself with the infants. 'Nanook!' he said; 'we'll call them Nanook!' He had heard the Elders say that it was unlucky not to name a baby. Then, as was the custom of his people, he slid on to a wrist of each baby a bracelet made of strips of plaited sealskin.

Atitak's sobs grew quieter and she became calmer. Anakattak, much relieved, fell asleep. When all was quiet in the village, Atitak got up. She picked up her sleeping babies, crept out of the igloo and walked through the icy polar night as long as she was able. Then she laid down the two Nanooks and slipped back to lie down beside her sleeping husband.

The babies cried and screamed but no one heard them. One of them crawled towards the icy sea. His brother made his way inland.

When Anakattak woke up he thought that the ice spirits must have taken his sons because their mother did not love them. Time passed, and Atitak had another son, Uluksak, and yet another, Awa. These were normal children just like all little Inuits. The boys grew up to become skilful hunters. One fine spring day, Uluksak left to hunt seal. Awa turned inland to follow the trail of a caribou. Neither returned to the village that night, and as days passed without a trace of them their parents believed that they must be dead. What had happened?

Uluksak was far out on the frozen sea when he heard strange noises as the ice around him cracked. It was too late for him to get back to the shore, and the ice on which he stood floated like a raft towards the open sea. Meanwhile, his brother Awa was also in trouble. As he crossed the tundra his dogs were frightened by wolves and ran off. Awa wandered about, unable to find his village, until exhausted, hungry, and hopeless, he fell asleep.

Uluksak was almost in despair when his ice raft crashed into a larger floe. He could see the entrance to a cave on it, and was about to seek shelter there when he came face to face with an enormous polar bear! He turned to escape but the animal seized him by his sleeve. Uluksak thought that his last hour had come, but the bear spoke gently to him: 'Don't be frightened; I am Nanook the polar bear, your elder brother. Eat some fish and I'll tell you my story.'

The next day, the wind changed. Nanook the polar bear made Uluksak get back on to his ice raft. As he said goodbye he gave him a tiny bracelet of plaited sealskin strips. 'Show this to our mother; she will know what it is,' said Nanook. 'Tell her that I forgive her.'

At just the same time, miles away, Awa opened his eyes. He felt deliciously warm and realized that he was under a blanket of thick, dark fur. Then the fur moved. It was a bear! 'There's nothing to be frightened of,' said the animal. 'I am Nanook the brown bear, your elder brother. Eat some meat, and I'll tell you my story.'

The next day, the brown bear led Awa back to the track leading to his village. As he left him, he handed him a little bracelet made of plaited sealskin strips. 'Show this to our mother. She'll recognize it, and tell her I forgive her.'

The two brothers returned to their village the same day. When they showed their mother the bracelets, she fainted. Since then, they say, bears and the Inuit belong to the same family.

*The brown bear set Awa on his homeward path.*

*For a time Arnaq lived happily with her new family.*

## GREENLAND

# ▷ THE TREACHERY OF ARNAQ ◁

For much of the day, Arnaq had been running across the tundra. Now, her strength spent, she could barely drag herself along. She had fled from her husband that morning, for she could no longer stand his anger and brutality.

At last she came to a solitary house in front of which hung the skins of polar bears. She decided to ask the people who lived there for shelter. Inside, a man and his two sons were eating their supper. They invited the woman to share their meal. They asked her no questions, not even where she had come from or where she was going. Seeing how tired she was, they made up a bed for her.

Arnaq fell asleep as soon as she snuggled under the thick fur covers, and did not wake up until the middle of the next day. She got out of bed, and looked through the narrow window of her room. She was terrified to see a polar bear, followed by two cubs, coming towards the house. At the threshold they stopped, and to her amazement they shed their skins to reveal her host and his sons. They looked up and saw her, upset to realize that she now knew their secret. They were humans inside the house, but turned into bears as soon as they went out. 'Now you know about us, you can never go back to live among humans,' said the father; 'you would never be able to hold your tongue, and hunters would come to kill us.'

At first Arnaq was happy, but as winter approached and the days became shorter, she became bored. She missed her family and friends, her village and even her husband, for she had forgotten his tempers and his cruelty. 'Let me go back,' she pleaded. 'I swear that I will never betray you.'

The father did not trust the woman, but the cubs were fond of her and hated to see her so unhappy. In the end they persuaded their father to let her go. 'Before you leave,' he said to Arnaq, 'swear again that you will never tell our secret. And remember that if you give us away, I will know at once, for bears know what humans are saying even when they are far away.'

The woman hugged the cubs one last time and set out for her village. Her husband, who was perhaps not as bad as she thought, took her back into his igloo. Every day he left to hunt with his dogs and sled. He dreamed of killing a polar bear, but he never found any tracks. Each evening, he came back in a worse mood. At last Arnaq whispered to him that she knew where he could find three polar bears, an adult male and two cubs. Her husband leaped into action, and as he harnessed his dogs Arnaq gave him directions. Whipping up his team, he sped off.

At the same moment, far away, the man-bear woke with a start. He knew that Arnaq had just betrayed them. He sent his cubs off towards the ice floes, telling them to run for their lives as far as their paws could carry them. Meanwhile, he set off towards Arnaq's village.

Arnaq was alone in her igloo when she heard a fearful noise as if the roof were falling in. Two vast paws closed round her neck, and she screamed so desperately that the other villagers woke up. When the bear left her igloo, he was pursued by furiously barking dogs and – more slowly – by the village hunters. But just as they came within striking distance of the bear, they were blinded by a shower of brilliant, coloured lights.

When they could see again, all was still and quiet. The bear and the dogs had disappeared. Looking up at the sky, the hunters saw that some new stars had appeared. They formed a new constellation, the Great Dog, which the Inuit think shows a pack of dogs surrounding a bear at bay.

And since that time hunters have known that they must be very careful before they set out after polar bears, for these mysterious animals can hear everything that people say!

FRANCE

# BRUN THE BEAR AND RENARD THE FOX

One beautiful morning, Renard the Fox left his den and knocked at the door of Brun the Bear. 'Sir Brun,' he said, 'I'm going to tell you a great secret.' Going close to the bear, the fox murmured confidentially: 'I know where to find a honeycomb as large as your head, full of the finest honey. I can't eat it all myself, and I thought you might like to share it with me.'

The bear's mouth watered as he thought of the huge honeycomb. He quite forgot that the

*The angry villagers and their dogs rushed furiously at the innocent Brun.*

fox had played many tricks on him in the past. 'Where is this treasure?' he asked impatiently. 'With Constant, the peasant who lives on the edge of the wood,' replied Renard. 'I've been watching the neighbourhood; it will be child's play to take it and there's absolutely no risk!'

Of course the fox was not the least interested in Constant's beehives, but in the chickens in his farmyard. He had raided them so often that Constant was becoming more and more watchful. So Renard had worked out a plot. 'If I am with Brun,' he thought, 'and we are seen, the bear is so huge that everyone's attention will be on him. They will run towards him and in the meantime I will easily be able to escape.

The two companions made their way to Constant's farm. By chance, the garden gate was open. They crept through it, and hid in a cabbage patch. 'We'll wait here until night,' advised Renard. 'We'd better run as few risks as possible.'

Although the bear was longing to taste the honey he thought this was a wise idea, since the hives were very close to the house. Renard looked across the cabbages to the farmyard where plump chickens were pecking about. The temptation was immense. He shut his eyes, but he could still hear the clucking of the hens. It was too much. He rushed over to the yard, seized the plumpest hen and carried her off. The other chickens rushed about squawking their heads off. They alerted not only Constant and his household but also all the neighbouring farmers.

'Run as fast as you can,' called Renard to Brun, who was still waiting in the cabbage patch. 'Shed your fur if it's too heavy, someone else will soon wear it for you! I'll go home and cook this chicken. What sauce would you like?' And with a peal of laughter, he raced off, leaving the bear to his fate.

When the peasants and their dogs saw the bear in the cabbage patch, they launched themselves at him. Sticks and stones rained down like hail on the poor animal. Brun thought his last hour had come, but desperation gave him the strength of ten, and he drove off his attackers. With a final effort, he gained the shelter of the wood.

Meanwhile Renard, who had seen the start of the fight from a safe distance, was happily gnawing Constant's chicken in his den.

*John and Mountain-Cleaver watched fascinated as Oak-Twister plaited treetrunks.*

FRANCE

# JOHN THE BEARMAN

Long ago a beautiful girl was carried off by a bear while she was collecting firewood in the forest. It imprisoned her in the cave where it lived, and before long she gave birth to a boy.

The boy soon grew tall and strong. Each day John, as he was called, struggled to push aside the giant boulder with which the bear blocked the cave entrance when it went out. At last the time came when he could push aside the rock. Mother and son hurried from the cave and ran at breakneck speed across the mountain. As night fell, they reached a village. When they saw John, the villagers cried out in terror, for he looked more like a bear than a human!

The two made their home on the outskirts of the village. The villagers soon accepted them, not least because John made himself useful. The villagers often asked for his help. He could carry the contents of a woodcart on his back, and reap as much corn in a day as an army.

One day John the Bearman, as he was known, decided to set out to see the world. He left the valley and the following day came to a large town. There a master blacksmith hired John as an apprentice. 'Straighten this ploughshare if you can,' he ordered his new apprentice. John did so at once, without even using a tool. The blacksmith next asked him to hammer out a red-hot iron bar. John took up a hammer and hit the bar so hard that the tool broke. He picked up a heavier hammer, and swung again. This time it was the anvil that split. The blacksmith realized that he would soon be ruined if John worked for him, but he let John make himself a huge iron walking stick before he left.

As he journeyed on, John heard a strange noise coming from the mountains on the horizon. When he drew near, he saw a giant beating the rock face with his bare hands. The cliffs were splitting under the blows. John asked the giant his name. 'They called me Mountain-Cleaver,' he replied. 'All my life, I have been opening up passes in these mountains.'

'Come with me,' suggested John the Bearman, 'and together we will be a match for anyone.' The two had been travelling together for some time when they came across a woodcutter, who was felling oak trees as if they were bulrushes. He stripped off their branches, and then plaited three trunks together into a cord. 'It's to tie my sticks with,' he explained to the astonished pair. 'I'm called Oak-Twister, and I'm collecting my winter wood.'

Oak-Twister joined the two friends and all three set out together. One day they came to a desolate region. The houses had shuttered windows, the people were wearing mourning, even the birds were silent. They asked a passer-by what was the matter. 'A devil has carried off our king's two daughters,' replied the man sadly, and added, 'their poor father has promised them in marriage to those who set them free.'

'Where does this fearful devil live?' asked the travellers. 'In a cursed castle in the middle of the mountains thirty leagues to the north,' said the villager. 'Here's work for us!' said John to his friends. And the three set out.

When they reached the castle, Mountain-Cleaver, whose walk had made him thirsty, quickly gulped down the water in the moat, and it was child's play for Oak-Twister to pull up the stakes that defended the castle's entrance and make them into a ladder with which to scale its walls. John used his heavy iron stick to break down the seven doors that guarded the great hall. The place seemed long abandoned.

'Mountain-Cleaver, come hunting with me,' suggested John. 'Oak-Twister, you light a fire and wait here for us.' Alone in the castle, Oak-Twister began to pile wood on the fire. Suddenly a hideous little monster tumbled down the chimney. 'It's the devil!' thought Oak-Twister. Before he could move, the fearsome creature struck his chest with the point of his sword and the giant fell asleep. When his friends returned Oak-Twister, ashamed of being taken by surprise by the devil, told them that he had fallen over a log and stunned himself.

The next day, it was Mountain-Cleaver who stayed in the castle. He too was put to sleep by the visiting devil, but he told his friends that he had slipped on the tiled floor.

Then it was John's turn to remain behind. He had not believed one word of his friends' stories. He stayed on guard, grasping his heavy iron stick. So when the devil tumbled down the chimney, John leaped up and struck him with all his might. But the devil's head was stronger than the blacksmith's anvil and he was only stunned. When he came to himself, he saw John lift his stick again. He begged for mercy, and promised to show John how to rescue the princesses.

'Come on, hurry up!' called John to his friends as soon as they got back. 'I know how we can rescue the princesses.' He raised the heavy hearth stone to reveal the top of a well. 'Here is a long rope. You go first, Mountain-Cleaver,' ordered John.

Mountain-Cleaver lowered himself cautiously down into the darkness of the well until the rope ran out. Then he called to his friends to pull him up. They tied on a second rope and Oak-Twister went down it. But at its end he too was left hanging in space. Was the well bottomless? They tied on their last rope. This time it was John's turn. After a seemingly endless descent in the dark, he found himself in a vast underground palace. With the help of his iron stick, he broke open several barred doors before he found the two princesses, fast asleep. Gently he woke them and sent them ahead of him up the rope to the castle.

When the princesses emerged from the well, Mountain-Cleaver and Oak-Twister thought of the king's promise. They cut the rope, abandoning John, and set off with the princesses. John, at the bottom of the well, furiously wondered how he could climb back to the surface. Suddenly he heard a quavering voice calling him. It was the devil, who could not bear to think of John living underground with him for ever. 'I know how you can get out of this hole,' he said, and gave a shrill whistle.

A giant white eagle swooped down. John climbed on its back and was swiftly carried up to the surface. He hurried to the castle of the king, who was preparing a feast for his future sons-in-law, Mountain-Cleaver and Oak-Twister. The two rascals fled as soon as they saw John, and the princesses welcomed their true deliverer with open arms. The king invited John to choose which of his two daughters he would like to marry. But John thanked the king politely, and went back to live with his mother.

*The devil begged for mercy as John threatened to strike him again.*

*The dogs barked at the enormous bear.*

SWITZERLAND

# THE CITY OF THE BEAR

Duke Berthold built a walled city at the foot of his castle to protect his people from robbers. When it was finished, he organized a hunt and decided to call his city after the first animal that was killed.

Around the city were forests rich in game, but all day the hunters saw neither deer, nor boar, nor wolf. When evening came they turned back, tired and dispirited. As they drew near the city, their dogs began to bark. The duke's horse reared up. In front of him, standing with one foot on a rampart, was an enormous bear. The duke jumped to the ground. Seizing a spear, he lunged at the bear's heart. But his blow missed, and the bear was only wounded.

The bear and the man struggled together. Berthold had only his hunting dagger in his hand, while the bear had powerful paws with sharp talons.The man felt the bear's hot breath, and the beating of its heart. He knew he was close to death but he felt respect for the wild animal, the kind of feeling he had for a worthy human opponent in a tournament.

Suddenly the bear relaxed its grip. The duke pulled free his right arm and struck a fatal blow at the animal's breast. Without even a groan, it fell dead. After a long pause Berthold turned towards his companions and said the one word 'Bear'. And this is how the Swiss town of Bern (which means bear) got its name.

## FRANCE

# THE DEVIL AND THE BISHOP

The devil was furious that Bishop Jacques of Tarentaise was building a new monastery. Taking the form of an enormous bear, he attacked the oxen of the peasants who were supplying the building materials until they were too frightened to venture on the roads. Without stone, work on the building had to stop.

Jacques realized that the devil was behind his problems, and decided to drive a team of oxen across the mountains himself. He made his way to the quarry from which came the best white stone, and left with his load. His cart was heavily laden, the path was stony, and the oxen plodded along very slowly. As night was falling, they entered a forest. Suddenly the oxen halted, bellowing with fright. A giant bear sprang forward, struck down one of them, and began to eat it.

The Bishop stood up in the cart and brandished his crozier at the bear. 'Do you think that you can prevent God's will? You must be punished for your boldness. I order you to take the place of the ox you have just killed.'

The bear was abashed. It dropped down on to all fours, lowered its head and penitently moved beside the second ox. The cart set off, drawn by the strange team. And from then on there were no more delays in the building of the monastery.

*The bear did as he was told.*

FRANCE

# VALENTINE AND ORSON

Queen Bellissant rode up to the edge of the great forest of Orleans. On its far side was the castle of her brother, King Pépin, whom she hoped would shelter her. Her faithless husband, the emperor of Constantinople, had thrown her out of his palace.

Bellissant was very tired as she entered the wood. She had to halt in a clearing and there she gave birth to twins, two lively boys.

The queen looked tenderly at her sons, and then fell asleep, only to be woken up by their cries. She opened her eyes to see a shebear disappearing into the trees with one of her babies. Without stopping to think, poor Bellissant sprang on to her horse and rode for help, leaving the second baby unguarded.

A few minutes later, King Pépin, who had been out hunting, rode into the clearing. The barking of his hounds drew him to the newborn baby, which was covered by a purple cloak pinned by a brooch of gold and ivory. The king thought the child had been abandoned, so he picked it up and carried it to his castle.

When Bellissant returned with some helpful woodcutters, she was appalled to find that her second son had disappeared. Mad with grief, she rode deep into the heart of the forest.

The first child, brought up by the shebear, grew up in the depths of the forest. He became an exceptionally strong youth, half man and half bear, for his body was covered with hair. Rumours spread through the region of a kind of monster, whom people called Orson the Savage, that menaced the countryside.

Meanwhile his twin brother, named Valentine by King Pépin, grew up at court. He became a brave knight and a skilful fighter, and the king looked on him as a son. When he heard that a monster lived in the forest of Orleans, he decided to go to find it. At dawn, without telling anyone, he saddled his horse and left the castle as quietly as possible. He rode for several hours until he reached the area where most of the sightings of the monster had taken place. The trees became so thick that Valentine had to dismount and continue on foot.

Suddenly his horse, which had been quietly following, reared up and neighed. Valentine seized his sword. In front of him he could see the monster holding a huge treetrunk as a club. The two stared at each other for a long time. At last, Orson gave a deep growl and launched himself at Valentine, who sidestepped him. One attack succeeded another but it seemed as if neither fighter wanted to strike a fatal blow. The fight went on and on.

At last Orson slipped clumsily and wounded himself on Valentine's sword. Instead of flinging himself on his oppponent, the knight ran to help Orson. As he staunched the wound, he spoke to him as to another man, and the monster seemed to understand.

Valentine took Orson back to court. The king gave him a room near that of Valentine, who began to teach Orson to walk upright, to talk, and to ride. He dressed him in man's clothes and one day the barber was called to shave off Orson's beard. Imagine his shock when he revealed the exact likeness of Valentine!

The young men often went hunting together. One day, they went so far that they lost their way. Luckily they came across a monastery where they took shelter. When the Mother Superior saw them she burst into tears and held out her arms to them. She saw, pinned on Valentine's chest, the gold and ivory brooch that he always wore. So Queen Bellissant had at last recovered her two sons, lost twenty years before in the forest of Orleans.

*Orson and Valentine fought each other, but their hearts were not really in the struggle.*

*The brave bullfinch lifted the twins out of the bear's reach.*

RUSSIA

# THE BEAR'S PRISONERS

As King Igor leant towards the stream to slake his thirst, an enormous bear appeared behind him, and seized him in its powerful paws. 'I will let you go if you promise me a present,' said the bear. 'I want you to give me a very precious possession from your palace, which you do not even know about.'

'I know every inch of my palace,' said Igor. 'What is it that you want?' The bear refused to explain, but the suffocating king was forced to promise. When he got home, Igor found that his wife had given birth to a boy called Ivan and a girl called Marfa. Now he understood the bear's words. He built a huge underground shelter and the little prince and princess grew up there in secret. Time passed and there was no sign of the bear.

A few years later, the king and his wife died on the same day. Soon afterwards the bear, thinking that the children were now large enough to be useful, came to the deserted palace. The bear was furious. 'Who will tell me where the prince and princess are hidden?' it snarled.

A strange knife, stuck into a wall, answered: 'Throw me into the air and watch well where I fall. Then dig at that spot.' The bear dug and dug until it reached the dwelling in which lived Ivan and Marfa. 'Your father wanted to deceive me,' growled the bear angrily. 'I will take you away with me and you will be my servants.'

The bear carried the two to the mountains where it lived. Ivan and Marfa had to cook its meals, light its fires, and clean its den. One day when they were on their own the children saw a falcon in the sky. They called it down to them and told it their troubles. 'Climb on to my wings,' said the bird of prey, 'and I will carry you far from here.'

Just as the falcon rose into the air with the children, the bear returned and saw them. It turned itself into huge flames that burned the falcon's feathers, and caused the prince and his sister to fall to the ground. A few days later, an eagle flew down towards them while the bear was asleep in its cave. 'Climb on my back,' the bird said, 'and I will carry you away from this country.' But the eagle had hardly reached the treetops when the bear sprang up. It turned itself into a flaming torch and burned the eagle's wings.

This time the bear wanted to kill the little prisoners, and only Marfa's tears made it draw back. The next day a bullfinch flew up to Ivan and Marfa as they gathered wood on the mountain. 'I know how you can escape from here,' it whispered. The children were astonished. How could a poor bullfinch succeed where a falcon and an eagle had failed? But they decided to trust the little bird, and with enormous difficulty it lifted them into the air. Before the bear could turn itself into flames, the bullfinch pierced a cloud with its beak. Huge raindrops soaked the bear and it retreated to dry off in its cave. The bullfinch struggled over the mountains with the twins. At last it reached a far-off country where Ivan and Marfa settled and lived safely for the rest of their lives.

FRANCE

# FIRST CATCH YOUR BEAR

In a little German village lived three great friends. They went from one inn to another, enjoying good wine, strong beer, and pretty girls. These three jolly rascals were happy with life but always short of money.

The owner of their favourite inn was sure that they would never be able to pay all they owed. He refused to give them any more credit, for they already owed him for many glasses of wine, flagons of beer and hearty dinners. 'Wait a bit longer, innkeeper,' they laughed. 'In two days' time we shall be as rich as kings. If you refuse to serve us today, you'll be sorry later.'

The innkeeper shrugged his shoulders. 'No one makes a fortune by hanging about the streets and amusing themselves from morning to evening. I can't afford to give you more credit. Times are hard for people like me. Travellers won't risk coming to our town since this cursed animal has been terrorizing the countryside. They say it is a giant bear, with the devil's own strength!'

The lads laughed at the innkeeper. 'This bear will make our fortunes,' they said. 'Its skin is worth its weight in gold. On top of the value of the fur there's a reward for capturing the beast. So serve up a good dinner, innkeeper! As soon as we've eaten, we'll set out to look for it.'

The innkeeper thought for a while. After all, what could he lose? Only the cost of three more dinners, and things were so bad that this would not make much difference. On the other hand, if the three rascals did manage to capture the bear, not only would they be able to pay their debts but his other customers would come back again.

And so the three companions were well fed when they set out to look for the bear. They came across it sooner than they had expected.

They had hardly entered the forest when they met the great beast face to face. They scrambled for safety, each thinking only of himself. The lightest seized a branch and swung himself up to safety in a treetop. The swiftest ran as fast as he could towards the town. The third, paralysed with fear, could only crouch on the ground. He held his breath, because he had heard that bears never touch dead things.

The bear stared down at him, and several times it batted him with its huge paw. It sniffed at him and finally – not taken in by his stillness – murmured something in his ear. Then it went on its way and disappeared into the forest.

The young man got up, pale and trembling. His companion, who had scrambled down from the tree, was fascinated by what he had seen. 'What did the bear tell you?' he asked. 'Amongst other words of wisdom,' replied the poor shaken lad, 'it said never to sell the skin of a bear while the bear is still running around!'

*The huge bear batted the rascal, as he played dead.*

# BEARS IN LEGEND AND REAL LIFE

The bear is a solitary animal. It likes to live alone and is not happy among other animals or in captivity. It is normally placid, but when it is caged it can become aggressive and dangerous.

### Clumsy beast

Its great size and hesitant movements can make a bear seem clumsy, as if hampered by its thick fur. But when necessary it shows great agility, easily climbing steep slopes and trees, and jumping obstacles over a metre high.

The bear normally moves on all fours, though it may stand upright on its hind feet to reach for food or to fight. When a bear runs, it ambles, lifting both paws on one side at the same time, rather than diagonally like a horse or dog. It can reach a speed of 50 kilometres an hour! It is also a good swimmer and loves to bathe during the hot summer months.

Bears are wanderers, moving round with the seasons or for no obvious reason. For safety, they mostly go out at night, and their poor sight is better adapted to darkness than to daylight.

### Clever hunter

Like humans, bears are omnivores. They eat meat as well as plant foods, such as roots, bulbs, berries and fruit. They are particularly fond of myrtles, blackberries (known in Scandinavia as 'bear berries') and the red fruits of the arbutus, sometimes called 'bears' grapes'. In autumn bears eat mushrooms, hazelnuts and chestnuts and are particularly fond of beechnuts. They scoop trout and salmon from mountain streams with their paws. But their very favourite foods are ants' eggs and honey.

The bear is one of the most intelligent mammals, with a well-developed sense of direction and a good memory. It is hard to track or to trap, and is a cunning hunter. If it is after sheep, for example, it will choose a moonless night or a foggy day, or may take advantage of a storm; and it avoids going back to a place where it has killed.

*A brown bear, subject of many myths and legends. This one is a grizzly bear from North America.*

### An endangered animal

The bear, like most other large mammals, is in danger. Its survival is doubtful in some regions, in particular in Europe where the numbers are declining alarmingly. Once bears lived over the whole of Europe. Now they live only in the Arctic and in a few mountainous regions in northern Europe, North America, South America and Asia. The destruction of forests and the increasing number of roads and other developments are destroying the last territories of the bears.

But efforts are being made to prevent their extinction. In Sweden and Norway strict measures to protect them have been taken, and their numbers have increased.

In the Arctic, the polar bear is also in danger as human activity increases in previously deserted regions and threatens its way of life. Although hunting is restricted and the sale of their skins forbidden, poachers are now tracking and killing polar bears from the air.

### The giant and the dwarf

There are several species of bear, which differ greatly in colour and size. The largest – apart from the polar bear – is the Kodiak bear, which can reach about 2.5 metres standing upright, and weighs around 800 kilograms. It lives on the Alaskan coasts. The grizzly bear, which has a much exaggerated reputation for ferocity, weighs no more than 500 kilograms. It is found mainly in the Rocky Mountains of the western United States. The 'dwarf' of the family is the Malayan bear, which weighs only 50 kilograms and is a metre long; it is also called the palm bear since it likes to climb trees. Because the bear is quite like a human in appearance, it features in many myths and legends.

*Once firearms became available, polar bears became easy prey for hunters. They are now protected.*

### Bears in prehistory

People have been fascinated by bears since earliest times, fearing them and respecting them at the same time. Their outlines were drawn on the walls of prehistoric caves, as part of rituals that took place before hunting. The bears in the pictures were very large, and would have been a serious danger to hunters armed only with bows and spears. But probably the hunters trapped the bears by driving them into pits. The huge cave bears disappeared gradually at the end of the Stone Age, when the climate grew warmer, and their place was taken by the brown bear.

*A black bear cub. Cubs look sweet but they can be very dangerous.*

### Artemis's animal

In Greek mythology the bear is often associated with Artemis, goddess of hunting. Brauronia, one of the oldest Greek sanctuaries, was built by the local people to appease Artemis when they had angered her by killing a bear. Very young girls known as arktoi (the Greek for bears) served as priestesses there. Every five years, a great ceremony took place in springtime, during which a she-bear was offered to the goddess.

Before setting out with the Greeks to fight the Trojans, Agamemnon intended to sacrifice Iphigenia, the loveliest of his daughters, at the sanctuary of Brauronia to make certain of a favourable wind. Artemis removed the girl, and replaced her with a bear.

Other Greek legends tell of children suckled and saved by bears. These include Paris, son of King Priam of Troy, who was abandoned at birth on Mount Ida, and Atalanta, left on Mount Parthenon by her father, who had wished for a son.

At about the same time, the Celts were worshipping the bear-goddess Artio. And in ancient Rome bears, mainly from Germany, were used in combats against other wild beasts and gladiators. The writer Petronius says that bears' paws were a delicacy much appreciated by rich Romans!

### 'Noble' game

During the Middle Ages, the forests and mountains of Europe were the home of many bears. In the 14th century Gaston Phoebus, the Count of Foix, wrote a treatise about hunting in which he described the different ways of attacking the animals: with a sword (unless it was very short), with a spear, with bow and arrow, or with a crossbow. He also described various traps, particularly one called a dardière in which the bear triggered a device which sent a very sharp spear into its side. Gaston Phoebus roundly condemned this practice as unworthy of a gentleman because, he said, the bear was 'noble' game which should be hunted with hounds.

Bears were much appreciated at court entertainments, where trainers made them dance and bound about.

### Polar bears

Polar bears were almost unknown in Europe and as a result were extremely valuable. In the 11th century an Icelander called Audhunn went to Greenland, where he gave his entire fortune for a live polar bear. He presented it to the king of Denmark who, to thank him, made him a cupbearer and gave him a pension for life. When the kings of Norway wished to honour a foreign king, they would send him a live polar bear.

### Dancing bears

Until the beginning of the 20th century, travelling entertainers with dancing bears were found all over Europe. They went from town to town dragging the bears behind them. Their arrival was always an event. The trainer would set up at a crossroads or in the market square and make his bear perform various antics to the sound of a drum. Onlookers were often dumbfounded to see the animal imitate humans so well. Later the bear would take its trainer's drum round for a collection. People thought that both trainer and bear possessed mysterious powers, and they were sometimes asked to heal illness. The bear would dance outside the sufferer's house to cure the sickness!

*This picture of a bear trainer comes from a 13th-century manuscript.*

*A bear hunt, from a 16th-century painting.*

In the village of Ercé in the Pyrenees mountains in France, there was even a 'bear school', unique in Europe, which specialized in training bears. This took 12 to 15 months and was carried out with considerable cruelty.

Dancing bears almost completely disappeared from Europe after World War I, apart from a few that linger on in the Balkan mountains.

### Hunting rituals

People of the far north of Europe and Asia, such as the Lapps and Siberians, did not think of the brown bear as an ordinary animal. Before they set out on a hunt they took numerous precautions to avert the animal's anger and prevent it taking revenge after death. They believed that a bear could hear what people were saying from far off, even when it was asleep, and so they avoided using its name; instead they referred to it by such phrases as 'the old furry one', 'the sacred game' or 'the old devil'. Some people, among them the Tatars, would not talk about their hunting tactics but communicated only by gestures.

When they came to the bear's den, the hunters woke up the animal before attacking it. After they had made their

*A hunter with a rifle outsmarted by a brown bear.*

kill, they sang and danced around it, praising their gods and thanking the bear for allowing itself to be killed. The bear's body was whipped with a birch rod to drive away evil spirits. The bear was taken back to the village the following day on a sled drawn by reindeer and a great feast took place. The leader of the hunt was given the most coveted meat, the bear's heart. When the feast was over, the bear's bones were carefully collected and buried. After three days, the customary mourning time in that region, the hunters purified themselves with ashes.

## An honoured guest

Similar hunting rites were found among the native people of Greenland when they hunted polar bears. There too the mourning period for a dead bear was the same as that for humans, three days for a male, five days for a female. The hunter took great care to avoid upsetting the soul of his victim. He treated the bearskin like an honoured guest. His wife would offer it water to drink and presents, particularly the soles of boots, since the bear was known to be a great traveller. They even told it stories. The Greenlanders thought that the bear would have such happy memories of its stay that it would tell other bears. Then these would come of their own accord to be killed, so that they too would be so honoured.

*Teddy bears make good friends and attentive listeners. Bears are a popular subject for children's stories The inset illustration comes from a 15th-century edition of* Aesop's Fables.

## The bear in literature

In the legends and stories of the Middle Ages, bears featured alongside lions and dragons as beasts confronting valiant knights. Less stately tales made much of the bear's greed. In *The Tales of Renard* Brun the bear is a greedy simpleton whose love for honey will lead him to do anything, and in several of the stories Renard takes advantage of this.

Many fables tell of bears. In *The Bear and the Lover of Gardens* La Fontaine denounces the stupidity of a bear which in trying to catch a fly perched on its friend's nose throws a heavy stone at his head. Even so, the storyteller shows the bear as an animal to be reckoned with.

Many stories tell of children brought up by bears; the legend of John the Bearman, half man, half animal, is found with many variations all over Europe. Christian tales associated the bear with the devil. When confronted by a saint, the beast becomes perfectly tame.

# INDEX